WHAT DO
WE MEAN
WHEN WE
SAY LOVE?

WHAT DO
WE MEAN
WHEN WE
SAY LOVE?

Compiled by Deidre Sullivan

Running Press   Philadelphia, Pennsylvania

CADER BOOKS

Copyright © 1993 by Cader Company Inc. and Deidre Sullivan.

Canadian representatives: General Publishing Co., Ltd., 30 Lesmill
Road, Don Mills, Ontario M3B 2T6. International representatives:
Worldwide Media Services, Inc., 30 Montgomery Street, Jersey City,
New Jersey 07302.

9   8   7   6   5   4   3   2   1
Digit on the right indicates the number of this printing.

Library of Congress Cataloging-in-Publication Number 93–83519

ISBN 1–56138–301–5

Cover design by Toby Schmidt
Cover illustration by Kate Brennan Hall
Interior design by Christian Benton
Edited by Melissa Stein
Typography: Adobe Garamond, with Bodega Sans,
    by Richard Conklin
Printed in the United States

This book may be ordered by mail from the publisher.
Please add $2.50 for postage and handling.
But try your bookstore first!

Running Press Book Publishers
125 South Twenty-second Street
Philadelphia, Pennsylvania 19103–4399

Acknowledgments

Many people have given graciously and generously in their time and thoughts in helping to provide this book with its tenderness and diversity. Thanks go to Seth Godin, Leona Gonsalves, Catherine Cook, Jerry Hubbard, Janet L. Nason, Ed. D., the Charlotte Christian School, Joyce Begnaud and the Academy of the Sacred Heart in Grand Cocteau, Louisiana, Nora S. Murphy and the Office of the Superintendent of Schools, Archdiocese of New York, Sister Dominica Rocchio, S.C. and the Office of the Superintendent of Schools, Newark, New Jersey, and Marcie Jerrell and the Convent of the Sacred Heart in Greenwich, Connecticut. Thanks also go to the United Way, especially the United Ways in Anchorage, Alaska; Bangor, Maine; Pulaski County, Arkansas; Bennington, Vermont; Seattle, Washington; Los Alamos, New Mexico; and Las Vegas, Nevada.

We're very grateful to Jeff Porten for all his help in accessing the world of computer networks. Special thanks go to Jeff Zaslow and his loyal readers who shared their thoughts with us for the book.

We also appreciate the support of Running Press, our publisher, and we'd especially like to thank our editor Melissa Stein, who helped us shape and perfect the manuscript.

At the core of this book is an essential question. To seek an answer to the mystery of what we mean when we say *love*, we reached out to a diverse group. We quickly reconfirmed that defining and describing love is a provocative, if not confounding, task. For although love is a universal experience, it is also the most personal experience of all.

Romantic love, filial love, parental love, puppy love, and the love that dares not speak its name—unfathomable, unstoppable, it comes in a thousand ways. Love we were told makes us laugh and reduces us to tears. It can make life worth living, and it can make life hell. Love can get us out of bed in the morning, and back into bed at almost any time. We long for it when it's missing, yet ache when it's there.

We gathered ideas about love in several ways. We talked with Americans of all ages and many walks of life. By posting information about this book on computer networks, we communicated with many others along the electronic highways interconnecting millions of Americans. Users of these networks sent through E-mail their descriptions, experiences, and metaphors of love.

Columnist Jeff Zaslow of the *Chicago Sun-Times* provided another valuable resource by writing about the "love book" and encouraging readers to contribute their thoughts.

When it came to getting in touch with children, schools across the country gave the project a boost. Many elementary-, middle-, and high-school teachers were gracious enough to pose our question as a homework assignment in their English and social studies classes. A handful of classes, in fact, created their own "love books" and forwarded them to us. Imagine our delight upon opening the mailbox to find a desktop-published book with these words emblazoned on its cover: *"LOVE by Mrs. Gribble's Third Grade Class"*! Outside the traditional school system, several homeschooled students also participated. Their contemporary thoughts are balanced with reflected wisdom from writers and philosophers of many other eras, providing a textured perspective.

The responses to our seemingly simple query open a window onto the emotional life of modern America. As you consider the answers to *What Do We Mean When We Say Love?*, you'll no doubt see some of your own ideas affirmed, and some challenged. Search your own heart or the heart of another—you'll find that whatever the answer, love is always a compelling question.

—Deidre Sullivan

Other languages have words to describe different states of love. I love my friend, my dog, my mother and my lover—but where are all the words to describe each specific state?

Kara Westerman, age 30
Actress and housepainter, New York City

There are more kinds of love than there are stars in the Milky Way.

James Baldwin (1924–1987)
American writer

Love is something that can be experienced every day—if you know where to look. Love doesn't have to be magical nor mysterious. A friendly smile from a stranger passing on the street is love. Love is not found only in hearts and cupids. Love is found in the concern for humanity we experience each day.

Michelle M. Walski, age 21
Chicago

Romantic love is when a person's thoughts of another's well-being occupy more time than the thoughts on one's own self.

Richard L. West, age 47
Chicago

The heart has its reasons which reason does not understand.

Blaise Pascal (1623–1662)
French mathematician and philosopher

Love is empty. It has to be in order to contain this infinite universe. . . . Try squeezing air in your hand. It escapes your strangling grasp yet fills your gasping lungs as it surrounds your living body. Love is empty. You're breathing it right now.

Mel Ash, age 40
Dharma teacher, Zen Center, Providence, Rhode Island

Love was being together and saying nothing. Love was when our silence spoke.

Anita Stein, age 63
Secretary, Skokie, Illinois

Love is like quicksilver in the hand. Leave the fingers open and it stays. Clutch it, and it darts away.

Dorothy Parker (1893–1967)
American writer

Love is letting a snake go after you catch it.

Chuck, age 7
Charlotte, North Carolina

What I know I know. What I don't, I don't. One thing I do know: love is at the heart of life. Love a woman, love a child, love a country—it fills your life.

Jack Nicholson, b. 1937
American actor

The most unique experience of love is the way one feels about one's kid. Up until I had a baby, at some level or another I'd been the center of my universe. When my daughter, Elizabeth, was born, that completely changed. I was telling my friend, Wendy, if a truck were coming and it was my daughter or me, I'd jump in front of the truck. Wendy said that's was a specious argument because trucks don't come and mow you down. I said forget the truck, it could be any kind of danger. My daughter's needs come first, and I think that until I had a child, nobody's needs ever came before my own.

Harriet Heller, age 52
Social services executive, New York City

If you sit on your mother's lap and lay your head on your mother's heart, you can feel your mother's love for you. You also feel safe.

Meredith Gombar, age 8
Charlotte, North Carolina

What do I mean when I say love (which is hardly ever)? Love is one of those really confusing things (like death and taxes) that constantly trips you up, no matter how smart you think you are. You can love your new go-go boots. You can love your brother. But there is nothing quite like that gut wrenching, sickening oh-god-I-just want-to-throw-up masochist's wet dream—it makes your head throb and your heart reel and your stomach spin. It clouds your judgement and warps your perception of reality. It's nasty and nauseating and quite often nefarious. Just can't get enough of it.

Cat Doran, age 28
Writer, New York City

One is very crazy when in love.

Sigmund Freud (1856–1939)
Austrian physician and neurologist

I'm no big fan of the love word. To this day I don't think I've ever said it to my husband, and I've been married for 18 years. To me love is just a word. You can say I love you, love you, love you. Love is action, what you do.

Sarah Poteete, age 35
Recreation specialist, Kekaha, Kauai, Hawaii

Love only finds you when you are minding your own business.

Dee Dee Isaacs Sturr, age 32
TV production executive, Phoenix, Arizona

Love is pure. Love is kind. Love is warm. Love is my mother, my father, my sister and my brother. Love is my cousin and my piano teacher; Love is my gerbil. Love is my friend Gale. Love is the miniature golf course at the beach. Love is the ocean. Love is winning a game. Love is my bike. Love is skiing in Colorado. Love is watching the Olympics. Love is trees. Love is playing tennis and missing the ball and then laughing. Love is eating ice cream. Love is going to the movies. Love is shopping. . . . Love is getting a good grade on a test. Love is God. Love is life.

Jennifer Chiurco, age 13
Princeton, New Jersey

Love is coming home from work at midnight to see a messy job of grass cutting in the head-lights—then discovering the next morning the words, "I LOVE U" cut into the long grass with the old push mower by my husband of thirty-six years who uses a cane to walk.

Coralina Stenstrom
Park Ridge, Illinois

Love is being there for somebody, totally being present, willing to listen, to do service if you need to, be there in a nonjudgmental sort of way, which sometimes is a lot easier said than done. In Yiddish, it's being a "mensch," a good person. That's what love is, trying to be a good person and living your life with integrity and to not be screwing people over. . . . It's all about being there for somebody else. For a long time we were in a society that was totally about "the self" and it doesn't work. It has to be about taking care of others, our community, our country and our world. If you want to find out about love, reach outside yourself.

Bert Bloom, age 46
Director of Shanti Project, a caregivers support program, San Francisco

Love is spending time with your family and friends before they slip away from you, right in front of your face.

Derek Wlasuk, age 12
Roselle, New Jersey

Love is my willingness to feel your pain in my heart when you have nothing to give in return.

Dale Kimball, age 65
Baptist Minister, Oak Forest, Illinois

There's "friendship love" which is where you can talk to a person but you aren't totally open. Then, you have "close friendship love" where the friend knows practically everything about you but there is still that part of you that they don't know about. Finally, there is "best-friend" love where you have a close bond with someone and you are like sisters. This person knows everything about you and your life and you don't hold anything back from each other.

Mirsada Pasalic, age 16
Larchmont, New York

Love to the Native American is all around us, each day of our lives. We love mother earth, the sky, the moon, the sun, the air, all living things on mother earth and life itself. Love is the gentleness in our parents and grandparents. The sparkle in the eyes of our children when they look at us. We cannot see or touch love, yet it is the strongest emotion we have. Above all, if you love yourself, your time on mother earth will be a joyous one.

T. Larson Medicinehorse Sr.
Crow Sundance Chief, Crow Agency, Montana

Love is like a garden. You've got to sow your seeds, make sure they get enough water, and nourishment, make sure they get enough sunlight, make sure you pull up all the weeds. You've got to toil the soil.

Billy Ray Cyrus, age 31
Recording artist, Nashville

When people hear that you are "in love" they never really take you seriously. I don't think it's true when someone says "She's too young to be in love." Love can happen at any age, at any time, with anyone. And once you are really truly in love with someone, you never forget that moment when you know you loved that person.

Katie Szymczyk, age 14
Charlotte, North Carolina

If we love someone, we must also say that we appreciate them in every way and love them for what they are, not what they could be.

Andrea Mitchell, age 18
Grand Cocteau, Louisiana

Love is not having your kindness taken for weakness.

Monica Dunford, age 37
Chicago

I came out of a family of Methodist and Presbyterian ministers. I was taught that love was something that you can only give away. If you gave it away you'd always receive it.

When I was growing up as a child my grandmother's stove was never cold. She cooked all the time. There was always food being cooked. Anyone who came by could always eat. Grandfather said that's sharing love. You are filling someone's stomach and helping them along the way.

I used to say I keep giving all the time and troublesome things happen to me and I'm always giving. Why? I wrote him a letter one day about this. He said I don't want you to ever question

God. When you begin to question God about what's happening to you, then you are going to doubt what he can do for you. As long as you don't question and keep on doing the things you are supposed to do, he'll give you the right answer. Keep giving. Always remember, the more you cast upon the ocean of love, the more that will come back to you.

Lilly Williams, age 66
Civil rights and community activist, Miami, Florida

An element of love is Trust. Our confidence in the one we love is constantly in question. Betrayal of a trust brings about malice, hatred, and a host of other problems. Therefore, when we say love, we say, "I am placing a degree of trust in you."

Abd Allah Matin, age 29
Inmate, Ossining Correctional Facility, Ossining, New York

t

To me, obligation is not love. Responsibility is not love. Letting someone be open and honest and free—that's love. It's got to be natural and it's got to come real.

Dolly Parton, b. 1946
American entertainer

Love is compromise. Deciding your need not to be alone is greater than your need to have things your own way.

Steven Birnbaum, age 24
Museum professional, Short Hills, New Jersey

Some people mistake infatuation for love. But for me, infatuation is more like a cold. It's three days coming, three days staying and three days leaving. When it's coming, you feel it taking hold of you. During those three days staying, it's as if you are so sick, you don't know if you will ever be normal again. But when it's over, you don't even remember how bad off you were.

Moira McLoughlin, age 26
Film production executive, Los Angeles

Nothing spoils the taste of peanut butter like unrequited love.

Charlie Brown
Cartoon character

It's the living together from day to day. . . . The long, slow enduring thing . . . that's what we live by . . . not the occasional spasm of any sort. Little by little, living together, two people fall into a sort of unison, they vibrate so intricately to one another.

D. H. Lawrence (1885–1930)
English novelist

One gains a profoundly personal, selfish joy from the mere existence of the person one loves.

Ayn Rand (1905–1982)
Russian-American writer

Love is anatomical curiosity and an artifact of biological consciousness.

Erik Kvam, age 34
Attorney, New York City

Love is an irresistible desire to be irresistibly desired.

Attributed to Robert Frost (1874–1963)
American poet

Love is the happy medium lying ethereally between one's own desires and others' expectations of you.

Tim Halpern, age 24
Actor, New York City

To love is to stop comparing.

Merrit Malloy
American writer

Love is only half the illusion; the lover, but not his love, is deceived.

George Santayana (1863–1952)
American poet and philosopher

It's like when the plane falls down really fast.

Zelma Davis
American musician

. . . Evian water and battery acid: when you mix the two you get love.

Kurt Cobain
American musician

I never liked the men I loved, and never loved the men I liked.

Fanny Brice (1891–1951)
American actress

. . . love is blind, and lovers cannot see
The pretty follies that themselves commit.

William Shakespeare (1564–1616)
English dramatist and poet

The arithmetic of love is unique: two halves do
not make a whole; only two wholes make a whole.

Joe Coudert
American writer

I have this theory about love. I think it's one of
the few, if not the only, emotions over which
humans have no control.

Rush Limbaugh
American television personality and writer

Love is when someone reaches down your throat—rips out your heart—takes it into the kitchen, chops it up into a thousand tiny pieces, shoves it into the oven and roasts it at 500 degrees for an hour. Then she serves it up to you on a silver platter and you're supposed to eat it and say, "Thanks honey, it's delicious."

Kjeld Erik, age 31
Musician, Bardonia, New York

Love is something that hangs up behind the bathroom door and smells of Lysol.

Ernest Hemingway (1899–1961)
American writer

Love is a delightful day's journey. At the farther end kiss your companion and say farewell.

Ambrose Bierce (1842–1914)
American writer

To live is like love, all reason is against it and all healthy instinct for it.

Samuel Butler (1835–1902)
English writer

Love is an unconditional surrender of affection.

William Mills, Jr., age 59
Advertising agency chairman, Atlanta

I think romantic love is unimportant, even destructive, and that we'd be better off as a society if we went back to marriages arranged by parents. My understanding is that societies where that's still the norm have fewer cases of impotence, fewer cases of infidelity, and fewer divorces. Moreover, fewer people report unhappiness in their marriages and on average, couples produce more children.

Nicholas Delona, age 35
Entrepreneur, Brockton, Massachusetts

First love is only a little foolishness and a lot of curiosity.

George Bernard Shaw (1856–1950)
British writer

Love is what happens to men and women who don't know each other.

W. Somerset Maugham (1874–1965)
English novelist

A man always remembers his first love with special tenderness, but after that he begins to bunch them.

H. L. Mencken (1880–1956)
American journalist

Love is like measles; we kant have it bad but once, and the later in life we have it the tougher it goes with us.

Josh Billings [Henry Wheeler Shaw] (1818–1885)
American humorist

The love we have in our youth is superficial compared to the love that an old man has for his old wife.

Will Durant (1885–1981)
American writer

The face of all the world is changed, I think, since I first heard the footsteps of thy soul.

Elizabeth Barrett Browning (1806–1861)
British poet

Love is patient and kind. Love is not jealous or boastful. It is not arrogant or rude. Love does not insist on its own way. It is not irritable or resentful. It does not rejoice at wrong but rejoices in the right. Love bears all things, hopes all things, endures all things.

The Bible: First Corinthians

In the past two years, love has been shown to me through actions. In February 1991, my daughter was still-born into my arms in my own bathtub. Love was the emergency room staff showing quiet respect and dignity with my wife and I in our intense grief. Love was women who had never told me of their similar experiences coming and hugging me through their own tears. Love was our families who got on airplanes that night to come and be with us. Love was a friend who called every week for a year just to see how I was doing. And because of those expressions I now know how to show love better. By shovelling the widow's walk up the street. And by hugging and holding a co-worker when his wife lost a baby last summer. And now, through some mystery beyond comprehension, being able to hold a new baby born on January 11th.

Steve Castro-Miller, age 32
Software executive, Sandy, Utah

Love can mean anything from true love like when you really love a boyfriend or girlfriend. Or you could say "I love my country" and this might mean that you are glad to be a citizen or happy to be here and not in a place like Iraq.

John Wilson, age 10
West Nyack, New York

Love is what you've been through with somebody.

James Thurber (1894–1961)
American writer

Love is caring for someone like you care about yourself and when something happens to them, you feel it too.

Noel Applebaum, age 31
Campaign manager, United Way, Las Vegas

Love demands infinitely less than friendship.

George Jean Nathan (1882–1958)
American editor and critic

What I cannot love, I overlook. Is that real friend-ship?

Anäis Nin (1903–1977)
French-born American writer

Love is when my dog jumps up on me and licks my cheek.

Bo Elledge, age 7
Charlotte, North Carolina

Love is patience for others, consideration, and respect. I work with elderly people who are sick and I think it's important to look at someone as a whole person, not just as someone who is ailing and needs help. Sometimes when people get old they aren't considered people anymore—but they are, very much so, and you can learn a lot from them. If you show them a little affection you'd be amazed at what they know. I've learned that most people are eager just to have someone show them some loving.

Aretha Barr, age 42
Nurses' aid, Orlando

I may not hear you when you call my name
I may not hear your voice through all the whirling
      noise and swirling echoes
I may not hear you're there
I may not hear you

    But if I do
    I'll hear the weave of your words
    I'll feel the shape of your thoughts . . .
    and it will be the most wondrous thing
      I know
    to hear that there is such a thing as you
      inside the world I know.

I may not feel you when you take my hand
I may not feel your touch through all the edges
      and vibrations
I may not know you're there
I may not feel you

    But if I do
    I'll hear the ocean in your heartbeat
    I'll feel the earth move in your breathing
    I'll trace the fountains of your feelings
    and it will be the most wondrous thing
        I know
    to find out that there is such a world as
      you out in the world. . . .

                Jim Sinclair, age 31
      Coordinator of an international network for autistic people

At the adoption center I work at, putting a baby in someone's arms who can't get a baby any other way is like Christmas, Thanksgiving, and Halloween and Easter and all the wonderful days of your life rolled into one experience. It's a big love experience. I never do it dry-eyed.

Judy Collier, age 42
Bangor, Maine

There is time for work. And there is time for love.
That leaves no other time.

Coco Chanel (1883–1971)
French fashion designer

i

It is trusting that your best friend will understand
someday why you asked an adult for help when
she tells you of her pregnancy at 15, again.

Kathleen Michelle McNeil, age 15
Grand Cocteau. Louisiana

Upon telling someone that I love them, I mean to say that I am available to them as needed within the margins of mutual respect, courtesy, loyalty, honesty, and thoughtfulness. I do not always expect to be loved back and that's okay depending on the relationship. Loving is a choice. I have not learned to love unconditionally and am not sure if anyone really does or can.

Stephanie Michelle Whitney, age 29
Junior high school teacher, Long Beach, California

I believe that as people we have diluted speech. We seem to have a penchant for blurring the meaning of terms and "love" gets particularly hard hit. When I hear, "Oh I love your suit," I cringe inside. I appreciate the compliment of course and appreciate the recognition even more, but since I presume that person would die for my suit, the comment feels out of place.

Bill Leach, age 45
Engineering consultant, Apex, North Carolina

Love is a score of zero in tennis.

Webster's New Collegiate Dictionary

The old art of romance needs to be brought back because so much of the mystery has been taken out of love. Back in Victorian times, a white rose meant purity, a red rose meant devotion, and a pansy meant forever. Presenting someone with a nosegay meant something and everybody knew that. But we've lost the symbolism of our gestures.

Maybe it's because we are overstimulated visually and sensually. People think if they watch loud music or watch television, that their senses and passions are being stirred; but they aren't. Maybe there should be a course in schools on how to love someone, how to respect someone, or how to have a marriage.

Lys Marigold, age 50
Writer, East Hampton, New York

I was married for 19 years to the man I fell in love with at the age of 16. He died suddenly last year and I now realize what our love was. I knew we were in love, and as I look back on our last year together, I realize that our love had come to its fullness. Love for us was being so much a part of each other's lives that we knew the wants, needs, desires, and thoughts of the other before they were spoken. I miss that feeling a great deal and wonder if I will ever experience it again.

Kathie Ewanio, age 42
Schiller Park, Illinois

Absence is to love what wind is to fire; it extinguishes the small, it enkindles the great.

Comte de Bussy-Rabutin (1618–1693)
French writer

When we love someone, our heart takes a picture of that person so we will always remember them. They will always be in the bottom of your heart. . . . My heart took pictures of someone I loved dearly who died at the age of 12. I will never forget him because my heart holds his picture.

Gina Spampanato, age 12
Stony Point, New York

Love is anterior to life,
posterior to death.

Emily Dickinson (1830–1886)
American poet

You can't work to get it. You must receive it and
then work to sustain it.

Chad Creed, age 13
Charlotte, North Carolina

Love doesn't just sit there, like a stone, it has to be
made, like bread; remade all the time, made new.

Ursula K. LeGuin, b. 1929
American writer

Love is about bringing out connections. It's about attending to and affirming that they exist in a range of ways. I've a tradition giving parties for my women friends. I got the idea eight years ago when I was turning 40 and going through a mid-life crisis. I was a single person; I had no children, and my work life was in transition. The traditional forms of community simply were not present in my life. I realized that my experience of life as a single woman was more like a maypole where I was connected by strings to many different people. After thinking through the concept of what makes community, I decided I would dub certain people here as my family and say that I was going to show all my facets to them. My vulnerabilities as well as my strengths, my pleasures as well as my sorrows. I was going to start acting like you are my local family. Friends said, "You are living a new model of community." It allowed me to begin to think, "well maybe so."

Deborah Swets, age 48
Consultant to non-profit organizations, Redmond, Washington

The love we give always is the only love we keep.

Elbert Hubbard (1856–1915)
American writer

My thoughts/feelings about love are closely related to my thoughts about God. . . . I believe in a completely benevolent, loving God; one who includes all the good qualities that exist, such as kindness, unselfishness, gratitude, joy, peace, etc. Perhaps the greatest, most potent and all-inclusive of these qualities is love. I also believe that, as Genesis says, we all are made in God's image. I believe it is our duty and purpose in life to prove that we are, in fact, God's image, and we do this by expressing His qualities as best we can.

This is the basis of my environmental attitudes as well. If I truly love the earth and all God's creations, I want to treat them with respect, kindness, understanding, and selflessness. The opposite of the qualities of God, and the opposite of love, are the root causes of environmental degradation: greed, hate, disrespect, unkindness, selfishness.

Jennifer C. Thomas, age 25
Graduate student in environmental policy, Ann Arbor, Michigan

I have a really strong love for my Muslim sisters, Muslim women. It's not a physical, or sexual thing. In fact, there are a lot of guidelines within Islam regarding the interaction between unmarried males and females: you can't be alone, there's no physical touching, etc. For example, I've never even touched my fiancé. We talk all the time. I'm getting to know her as a partner, as a Muslim sister. It's more of a spiritual and emotional relationship, one that is based on respect.

Jowaad Abdul Rahman, age 21
College student, Cincinnati

Love is not the universal brotherly affection which we all try to make it. I don't particularly trust that people really want to love their neighbors. I'd be happy with a cordial, mutually respectful relationship with my neighbors.

Philip Birnbaum, age 28
Marketing executive, New York City

When my sisters and I were growing up in Berkeley, California, my mother tried to show us that through simple gestures of beauty we can express love and appreciation for our neighbors. So every year on the first day of May, she would get up early in the morning to help me and my sisters make little baskets of flowers which we then quietly left in the doorways of our neighbors' homes.

Sophie Hahn, age 31
Attorney, New York City

Love equals benevolence plus affection plus doing good acts plus generosity. In reference to the opposite sex, add devotion to that sum.

Ethel Brown, age 62
Coding analyst, Kansas City, Missouri

Sometimes strangers show love in unexpected ways. Once on a flight from New York to Dallas, right before takeoff, I got very nervous. I was almost trembling. I tried to get over my fear by chewing gum, reading a magazine, and listening to relaxation tapes all at the same time. The man sitting next to me asked what was wrong and I told him that air travel made me very uncomfortable. When the plane began to taxi for takeoff, he offered to hold my hand and let me put my head on his shoulder. He also took the time to explain every sound, every roar that the plane was making so that I'd understand what was going on around me. He didn't let go of my hand or stop talking until the plane was safely in the air. To me, this kindness to a stranger was love in action.

Mary Ann Reed, age 44
Fashion executive, New York City

Love is holding a friend's hand.

Kristen Huey, age 6
Charlotte, North Carolina

Greater love hath no man than this, that a man lay down his life for his friends.

The Bible, John 15:13

There's a lot to be learned about love from animals because they demonstrate unconditional love. It's something that a lot of humans need to learn. Animals give love and ask nothing in return really. Their love is so honest. It's very simple, but very steadfast. My own animals are very sensitive to when I'm hurting or sad.

Once I rescued a calf from a dairy and I slept with it the first night because it was so scared and so sick. The next day he followed me around like his own mother. You could just see the gratitude in his eyes. Among the animals I've taken from abusive situations, their ability to love again is amazing. They are so grateful and so forgiving.

Diane Danielson, age 42
Coordinator, traveling youth environmental performance group
Portland, Oregon

Love is being nice to my gerbils.

Thomas Huckaby, age 6
Charlotte, North Carolina

When we say love, we are saying that we love each other for fear that God won't love us.

Carlton Ficklin, age 26
Inmate, Ossining Correctional Facility, Ossining, New York

I can see the stars in the eyes and smell the trees in the aroma of a person who loves nature and spends time there. People who love God take on a divine sort of serenity. People in couples take on the expressions and the attitude of each other and those who love life carry with them a certain vitality not seen in others. Whatever it is, love shapes you and so to say the word "love" in connection with anything or anyone is to acknowledge that thing or that person as a part of who you are.

Elizabeth McQuitty, age 17
Grand Cocteau, Louisiana

In our life there is a single color as on an artist's palette which provides the meaning of life and art. It is the color of love.

Marc Chagall (1887–1985)
Russian-born French painter

Love is a matter of heart and mind, materializing through the soul. The soul has no boundaries, and through the heart and mind, it reveals love.

Mary L. Witkin, age 82
Ridgewood, New York

Love is the greatest magic there is.

Selena Fox, age 48
Neo-pagan priestess, Mt. Horeb, Wisconsin

To fall in love is to create a religion that has a fallible God.

Jorge Luis Borges (1900–1986)
Argentinian writer

Sometimes love is stronger than a man's convictions.

Isaac Bashevis Singer (1904–1991)
Polish-born American writer

Reality is extremely valuable in love. What I mean is this: when we love someone as he or she really is—faults, limits, and all, love stands a better chance of lasting. To the extent that we idealize the person we love, we introduce possibilities for disappointment and difficulty. Seeing each other realistically in no way need dilute romance; in fact, it is a definite enhancer of the real thing for the real person.

Theodore Isaac Rubin, M.D.
American physician

A relationship with Rosie is not a game. It's a full-time job. The rest is a weekend deal, like the National Guard.

Tom Arnold
American actor

Love is the point at which one can accept a person for what they are and feel compassion for them even though they may not be perfect.

Laura Frugé, age 17
Grand Cocteau, Louisiana

I married my first husband because I loved him despite everything. For more than ten years I loved him despite his alcoholism, despite his occasional physical abuse, and despite his general ill temper. When his behavior grew so oppressive that even I couldn't love him anymore, he moved on to another victim. Several years later, I married someone who had become my best friend. He didn't drink, he was totally non-aggressive, and he was the most rational person I'd ever met. I didn't love him despite his behavior, I loved him because of his behavior. You've probably heard that story a thousand times already. There's a lot to be said for maturity, experience, wisdom, ad infinitum.

Linda Dunn, age 40
Computer specialist, Greenfield, Indiana

Love is not enough. It must be the foundation, the cornerstone, but not the complete structure. It is much too pliable. Too yielding.

Bette Davis (1908–1989)
American actress

I think that we all should pick one thing we really could love and care for and just love it and care for it as much as our human hearts can take.

Jennifer A. Griffin, age 10
Stony Point, New York

When I think of love several words come to mind. The first is "feel." If you love someone you feel with them. I don't mean you live through them but their feelings influence yours. I also think of the words "more important" meaning you put those you love ahead of yourself. You don't focus on how their situation affects you but how it affects them. The next word is "strength." I think most people have strength for their loved ones beyond what they thought. Sometimes that strength means going against their wishes or even absorbing their anger. The other word is "open," the idea of allowing yourself to be open to pain and loss. At Shanti, we're open to pain not because we are masochistic but because we care for the people we work with enough to be willing to stick with them through the rough parts. The last word is "acceptance." If you love someone you accept them as they are and who they are, unconditionally if you can. Accept what is there. I've learned about love from my husband, my friends, my co-workers and the many people in my life I've lost to AIDS.

Norma Barsness, age 71
Volunteer, Shanti Project, San Francisco

Love cures people—both the ones who give it and
the ones who receive it.

Karl Menninger (1893–?)
American psychiatrist

I love the Earth and the Earth is kind of like a
friend to me. Sometimes I talk to the Earth for no
reason at all. I tell it what I've been feeling, what's
going on. You know how some people say that
you should treat the planet like your mother?
When you say something really mean to your
mother she punishes you. We've been polluting
the Earth for a long time, taking its resources, and
now it's pooping out on us; it's like a punishment.

Amy Danielson, age 9
Portland, Oregon

Love is sharing with people who aren't your best friends. Love means that you don't bother animal eggs. It also means to say you're sorry to people that you might accidentally hurt. Love is not hitting people on purpose.

Charles Howard, age 7
Charlotte, North Carolina

Love is what I see every day in my working life. I work at an adult care center where we provide for functionally impaired adults. Love is the care given to people who cannot care for themselves by professional staff from the nurses down to the aides. The staff certainly doesn't do this for money because these jobs don't pay that well. To help someone go to the bathroom or to feed them or to wipe their chin when they are drooling shows a real love for mankind and real caring for other human beings. Seeing this in my life everyday, I think, has made me a better person because I'm able to take part in that kind of an atmosphere. In an atmosphere of caring, love is contagious.

Mary Joe GreenLee, age 54
Director, Holly Hock Adult Care Center, Las Vegas

What do we live for, if it is not to make life less difficult for each other?

George Eliot [Mary Ann Evans] (1819–1880)
English writer

Love is giving your last dime to the poor box.

Nicholas Lemesis, age 7
Roselie, New Jersey

During Hurricane Iniki, it was very emotional. I was sitting there with my son, my husband and my grandma and all I could think about was if I would make it out alive and would I live through this and boy am I really gonna change. Thought about love for my family and a lot about some of my friends who have died recently and my love for them and how much I missed them and . . . I might be joining them in that zone wherever they are.

Corinne Brandt, age 32
Teacher, Kekaha, Kauai, Hawaii

The most important love in my life is the unconditional love I'm learning to give to myself. I was
always looking for an outside source of love to
fulfill a basic need, while what I was searching for
in others was right there inside of me. Discovering
I was HIV positive has forced me into looking for
love from the inside. If I'm to beat HIV and I'm
doing it now, my strength has to come from me. I
still have a long way to go because I'm not quite
sure yet what this unconditional love for myself
means. As I can fulfill this love, my sense is that
everything else falls into place.

Spinner, age 40
AIDS activist and artist, Eugene, Oregon

The greatest happiness in life is to love and be loved in spite of ourselves.

Susan Jordan, age 36
Coon Rapids, Minnesota

To love oneself is the beginning of a life-long romance.

Oscar Wilde (1854–1900)
Irish-born English writer

Love is being nice to other people even if you don't know them.

Abby VanDerVeer, age 9
Charlotte, North Carolina

Love your enemies in case your friends turn out to be a bunch of bastards.

R. A. Dickson
20th-century writer

I know nothing about Platonic love except that it is not to be found in the works of Plato.

James Agate
English critic

Love is a grave mental disease.

Plato (427–347 B.C.)
Greek philosopher

Love is like an elephant so grey and massive, full of antiquity and memory. Hunted down for its hard white elegant tusks. Feared and respected. Enslaved in marvelous circuses. Accompanied by other freaks: the person with no limbs, the sword swallower, the geeks, the lion trainer, the clowns. And why should so marvelous a creature have the stigma of being afraid of a mouse?

Anonymous
Written on the kitchen wall at a party in New York City's East Village

The right setting can help make love happen. I fell in love one October night on Ocean Parkway in Brooklyn. I was with this guy, an artist from Germany, and we were driving in his old huge convertible with the top down. I was lying down on the front seat with my feet hanging out the window and we were going really fast. The air was rushing all around us. We felt very free. It was a perfect night for romance.

Catherine Cook, age 29
College administrator, New York City

My favorite kind of love is what I call "new love"—my personal mixture of "puppy love" and "lust." It's that feeling you get when you first meet someone and discover you have things in common, and things to say to each other, and stories to tell. It is when you find someone who actually *wants* to hear all your stories, and that's great because everyone else in your life has heard them a thousand times before. New love is when you find someone that you start thinking about every minute of the day and night, when thoughts of them can override and diminish all thoughts of your current life and situation. And believe me, this can be *very* dangerous. . . .

Anonymous
Seen on CompuServe, a computer network

In love there are two things—bodies and words.

Joyce Carol Oates, b. 1938
American writer

Although there's a case to be made for an occasional one-night explosion of passion, the only
thing that makes sex extraordinary is love. Period.
Forget the carnal mythologizing.

Debra Winger, b. 1955
American actress

The difference between sex and love is that sex relieves tension and love causes it.

Woody Allen, b. 1935
American filmmaker and actor

The basis of monogamy is not sex. It is acknowledgment of the sanctity of a core connection.

Toby, age 29
Graduate student in human development

One day he came over and I was taking the extensions out of my hair and Tony didn't even flinch. He'd just sat down and started helping me. I always wanted to find a man who would love me between touch-ups—not just when I'm glamorous. And when Tony loved me in my most natural state, I knew I found my special soulmate.

Vanessa Bell Calloway
Actress, Los Angeles

When I say love, I mean being faithful, loyal, kind, willing to risk something for a person. I call this the triangle of love. If you take one part of the triangle away, you don't have love.

John Frawley, age 9
Stony Point, New York

I think of love as a muscle like the heart. It's powerful. It pumps blood through you and keeps you alive and feeling good.

Amanda Innis, age 12
Princeton, New Jersey

The Simpsons has a lot of attributes that families can identify with, like loving the people that you want to strangle. . . . Families are about love overcoming emotional torture.

Matt Groening, b. 1954
American cartoonist

Growing up a Chinese American (I was the first in my family to be born in this country), I have had to straddle east and west. From the east come the Chinese virtues of familial love: respect for your parents, reverence for your elders, and responsibility for those younger than you. When I say I love my family, it is intellectual and rational. However, for me, "loving" someone not related to me has a more "western" definition. It is emotional, and not always rational, with a strong feeling of being soulmates with someone and caring about them. Loving an individual is not something that comes easily, and is never something to be toyed with.

Christine Wu, age 23
Technical writer and office manager, Milwaukee

When we were born we were given a big bag of loves. Everyone has the bag but some don't know how to open it.

Devon Wilson, age 15
Wilton, Connecticut

I am the mother of a severely disabled child. I think the greatest love that I've experienced is the unanticipated joy of ordinary life with this adolescent. The moment that comes to mind is one when he came home from school and he was jabbering about what went on that day. Then he went to his room and I heard him calling a friend and making plans for the weekend. I was fixing a cup of tea and staring out the window and found myself truly surprised by the love and joy I felt at this totally ordinary moment that we were given in a life that has sometimes been very hard.

Jane Johnston, age 45
Graduate student, Hopkins, Minnesota

Love never fails and doesn't keep records.

Annie Archer, age 11
Charlotte, North Carolina

My parents are the two most in love people I've ever known and I've learned a lot from how they live their lives together. For example, after I was born, my mom wanted to go back to work. At that time, my dad had just gotten out of law school and started a job. He told his employers he wanted to take some time off to care for me and the message he got back was, "quit or be fired." So he decided to quit and put his career on hold. The fact that he was willing to make that sacrifice so that my mom could work, to me, is very cool and very loving.

Rachel Hirsch, age 18
Belmont, Massachusetts

My sister Stephanie just got married, and at the rehearsal dinner her fiancé, Tim, presented her with a book of poems that he'd written about her. Tim is an English teacher and poetry is his art. My sister and Tim had been going out for about a year and a half and apparently, he'd been writing poems about his love for my sister throughout the entire time they were dating. The book was bound in leather and really beautiful. I thought it was an incredible act of love that he chose to show his devotion to Stephanie through his writing.

Julie Brown, age 21
Chicago

Love is like a piece of fruit—there are many kinds. A banana may be brotherly love. An orange could be love of your parents. An apple may represent the love of children, a blueberry could symbolize sisterly love and a plastic piece of fruit could be false love with no meaning.

Roopa Nalam, age 11
Grand Cocteau, Louisiana

Love is also like a coconut which is good while it is fresh, but you have to spit it out when the juice is gone, because what's left tastes bitter.

Bertolt Brecht (1898–1956)
German dramatist

Love is a fruit in season at all times and within reach of every hand. Anyone may gather it and no limit is set. Everyone can reach this love through meditation, spirit of prayer, and sacrifice, by an intense inner life.

Mother Teresa, b. 1910
Roman Catholic missionary

There are times when I can't stand it. I just look at him and I go, "Oh my God! Heart be still."

Oprah Winfrey, b. 1954
American talk show host

Love is so much better when you're not married.

Maria Callas (1923-1977)
American singer

My most brilliant achievement was my ability to persuade my wife to marry me.

Winston Churchill (1874-1965)
British statesman and writer

When I'm in love, it's about poetry and intensity and romance. . . .

Kyle MacLachlan
American actor

It is love that asks, that seeks, that knocks, that finds, that is faithful to what it finds.

St. Augustine (354–430)
Church father and writer

I think a man and a woman should choose each other for life, for the simple reason that a long life with all its accidents is barely enough for a man and woman to understand each other; and in this case to understand is to love.

William Butler Yeats (1865–1939)
Irish poet

Love is that which flows from God
Into my being
Through my arms and out my hands
To touch the person I am with.

It is this love that connects us
Deeply to each other
So that we are one.

In love, one being.
Together, one with the oceans,
And one with the stars in the sky.

In this love,
We are at peace
In ourselves
And with God.

Stephen Harding, age 37
Massage therapist and seminarian, Brooklyn

Love is sitting by a warm fire drinking hot chocolate and giving hugs and kisses to your parents.

Bo Stiles, age 9
Charlotte, North Carolina

They say love and chocolate tickle the same pleasure centers in the brain. Well, now that I've got love, I don't need chocolate.

Elizabeth Taylor, b. 1932
British-born American actress

There is no love sincerer than the love of food.

George Bernard Shaw (1856–1950)
British writer

I was one of those kids who was highly pressured into taking music lessons as a child by my parents. I persevered because deep down inside, I loved everything about music—the preparation, the performance, the pain that goes into development, and mostly the sounds that reflected perfectly the vicissitudes of life. When I went to college, I began as a Pre-med major, planning on following in my father's footsteps. Somewhere along the way, I felt an enormous emptiness, which I soon realized was the fact that I could not live without music as a major part of my life. My decision to pursue music at the expense of huge parental disapproval is the biggest decision I've made in my life. I could not have done so without an intense love of music.

Daniel Lau, age 26
Doctoral student in piano, Baltimore

Ever since my son was around eight, big enough to know that Santa Claus wasn't the one to fill his stocking on Christmas, he took it upon himself to make sure that I'd always get a stocking too. Twenty years later he still does the same thing and no matter where I'm living, he gets me my stocking. One Christmas Eve, for example, I was sound asleep and he let himself into my apartment. I was living alone at the time and the apartment wasn't decorated for the Holidays so he snuck into my room and found a panty hose and filled it with stocking goodies. When I woke up the next morning, there was a stocking for me. I can't tell you how surprised I was and how happy it made me feel. It was a very special act of love.

Fern Daily, age 60
Upland, California

Love is teaching other people's children all day long, coming home drained, and finding the energy to drive my son to where he needs to go. Love makes me forget about my tiredness.

Sandra Rulle, age 42
Art teacher, Miami

Someone that doesn't experience a love of some sort has an emptiness in their life that cannot be filled with any other emotion.

Nicole Fontanella, age 17
Armonk, New York

It's maintaining the friendship and taking the responsibility of being a friend and also helping the other person be a friend to you, and expressing your feelings about your friendship. Stephanie [Seymour] and I do that with each other. It's a good thing.

Axl Rose, age 31
American rock singer

Love is never needing to hold back what you feel and say.

Carol Gonsalves, age 51
Concord, California

Love is sex without a condom.

Nina Sullivan, age 27
Greenwich, Connecticut

It's been a lot of work and effort, but I think my marriage the most satisfying and greatest accomplishment of my life. I think that my wife knows me in ways that others don't including my mother and father. She knows the best parts of me, and the worst parts. For someone to still tolerate and love and like me after all those years, it is sort of a reflection that I'm not as unlovable as I think I am.

Michael Duxler, age 38
Mental health professional, Los Alamos, New Mexico

If you're in love with somebody, you have a particular vocabulary with that person that you have with no one else, a physical and verbal vocabulary that is unique.

Annette Bening
American actress

When I was in the military they gave me a medal for killing two men and a discharge for loving one.

Tombstone of Leonard Matlopich
Air Force Sergeant, Congressional Cemetery, Washington, D.C.

We are so trained in the thought system of fear and attack that we get to the point where natural thinking—love—feels unnatural and unnatural thinking—fear—feels natural. It takes real discipline and training to unlearn the thought system of fear.

Marianne Williamson, b. 1953
American writer and spiritualist

I think love is when you incorporate someone, or something, into your definition of who you are. Where that someone, or something, becomes part of your identity and self-definition.

Todd Jennings, age 33
University professor, Developmental Psych and Education, San Bernadino

Love Is Like Oxygen.

Song title, by Sweet

Love is a friend who cares and shares, a friend who speaks from the heart and always tells the truth.

Angela Johnson, age 10
Charlotte, North Carolina

My life experience has been that love is a decision to be faithful to a person. For me, as a Catholic Christian, it's a basic fidelity to the other, to God and all that that relationship involves. I think when we're young there's a lot of emotion in love, but there's a different kind of emotion involved in being faithful. It comes out of the gut, out of a promise to a person. I work at a shelter for teenagers so for me love means being faithful to the kids. When these kids arrive on our doorstep, they are hurt. They often don't know what love means. When a kid comes to the door, it's as if God is saying, "I love this kid. Would you love her for me so she can know I love her." We give unconditional love to the kids even when they act out or throw things or when they are verbally abusive. The unconditional love can teach them that it is possible to love people as they are. That's why it's difficult because you often don't get anything back. It's like hugging a pincushion.

Arlene Boyd, R.S.M., age 54
Director, residential home for teenage girls, Anchorage, Alaska

Love has nothing to do with what you are expecting to get—only with what you are expecting to give—which is everything.

Katherine Hepburn, b. 1909
American actress

Love is a quality that everybody has within them and I think it comes from God. We all have love and the ability to express it in our own unique ways. I think there are unique ways you love your boyfriend; there's a way to love children. You can have a great love for your job, or your life. I think it's a quality that comes out in a lot of different ways but its source is a spiritual love.

Caroline McClure, age 25
Public relations professional, Redmond, Washington

My experience of God's love is when I succeed in something special where I have been making a great effort. I also experience God's love when I make up with people. Making up is like a miracle.

Makiko Goda, age 14
Greenwich, Connecticut

If you don't have it, a part of you is missing.

Amanda Ferguson-Cradler, age 10
Portland, Oregon

Love ceases to be a pleasure when it ceases to be a secret.

Aphra Behn (1640–1689)
English writer

Keeping love to yourself is as painful as losing it.

Mark Magner
Graphic designer, Tarrytown, New York

There's exciting, physical attraction, fast, happy kind of love that young folks experience and I suppose we all do; I do. It resulted in my marriage to my wife with whom I've had a wonderful relationship for 41 years. That kind of love gives way over the years to a kind of trusting, respectful, dependable kind of love on which the partnership builds in the later years.

Cliff Eames, age 65
Retired business executive, Bangor, Maine

No man or woman really knows what perfect love is until they have been married a quarter of a century.

Mark Twain (1835–1910)
American writer

Respect has a lot to do with love. Without respect, true love is not possible. Whether it is love for the earth, for family, for friends, or for a companion, it is not love without respect. If you love the earth, you respect it by taking care of it and watching out for its well being. If the love you feel towards your family is true, you will respect their beliefs, ideas, and their individuality.

Megan McAvey, age 15
Weston, Connecticut

Love is where you see that you and the other are connected. I see love as the glue that holds everything together—it really is already together so when you experience love, you know what exists.

Although we'd written each other for a year prior to meeting, I decided to marry my husband on our first date. He proposed on the way to the restaurant where we were going for supper. I accepted and ten days later we were married. We waited those ten days because it took that long to get the church.

Now we've been married 25 years. Love is what we've created out of that knowing. We've created the love within the container or the structure of the knowing that we were to marry. I know that sounds awfully mystical, but the usual way of thinking about romantic love is that you fall in love and figure out why you are together. In a sense that relationship exists and you create the lifelong love within it.

Our myths of romantic love are very limiting. There aren't many myths in this culture about long-term committed love and we've got to come up with new myths for marriage. The myth of romantic love leaves us in the first stage of love. Then you get all these questionnaires in the dentist's office about how much spice your marriage has and all these things. These questionnaires are all predicated on a kind of first level loving, but not on the different stages people go through. Everything seems to say either you are in love or out. We have developmental myths of personal growth but not one for love.

Because we don't have a developmental myth all we've got are people falling in love, getting married, and then becoming terribly disappointed thinking they chose the wrong person.

Betty Sue Flowers, age 45
Professor of English, Austin

Because I'm in a wheelchair, I have become acutely aware of what other people need partly because I need so much myself. I need help with the shower, getting dressed, and getting to work. That's a lot for someone to do. I'm not able to provide those services for someone else, nor would they want me to. So I have to try to be very aware of other individuals and where people's different needs are connected. In most of my relationships that have developed from someone doing me a favor to me doing a favor for that person, there's a basic exchange of values. But in a true loving situation, that value is no longer exchanged evenly. Love may be in a sense what balances out the whole equation.

Jason Tweed, age 24
Writer and lecturer, Philadelphia

We can only learn to love by loving.

Iris Murdoch, b. 1919
Irish writer

I remember reading Sartre's *Nausea* as a college student and coming away with the sense that Sartre was right: Loving humanity is impossible. Now I know that Sartre was wrong. If love is only affection then Sartre was right: it's impossible to conjure up feelings of affection for everybody. But it is possible to love everybody, if by love we mean—as I do—acting out of concern for others.

In the end, I guess I'd simply say that love isn't a noun; it's a verb. It's not a feeling; it's an action. Thinking about, and then acting for others.

Will Swaim, age 36
Magazine editor, Newport Beach

Love conquers all.

Virgil (70–19 B.C.)
Greek poet

A year ago a couple in our community had a child and the child died of sudden infant death syndrome. The couple was, of course, devastated. There was a tremendous rallying of support for these people. One thing I can remember was about three days after it happened, about 50 people came to their farm in January and we walked the long lane down to their house. We all had candles. There were parents and children—a lot of different types of people from the community. We surrounded their house and just stood there. They could see us; we told them we were coming and that they didn't have to come out if they didn't want to. For a long time we just stood outside in a circle around their house with the candles so that they knew that we were thinking and trying to help them through this hard part. The message we were sending was: though this terrible thing happened to you, you have a tremendous circle of love around you, people who care about you and want you to see your life beyond this moment because your life is bigger than this tragedy. You are more than your sadness.

Heidi Swets, age 40
Decorah, Iowa

If we really love a person we leave that other person space to grow and to develop within the framework of his or her goals.

Beth Cheadle, age 58
Social services supervisor, Manchester, Vermont

Let me not to the marriage of true minds
Admit impediments. Love is not love
Which alters when it alteration finds,
Or bends with the remover to remove.

William Shakespeare (1564–1616)
English writer

At my age, love is a young woman called Nostalgia.

George Bushulen, age 55
Nashville

I find as I grow older that I love those most whom I loved first.

Thomas Jefferson (1743-1826)
American President

The more experience I have, the more clear it is love is a decision to feel a certain way. It's not something that is dependent on how another person is, or who another person is, what they are or how they respond to me. It's a decision of how I'd like to feel about them. A friend of mine says that love is like the sun, it shines on everybody. If you want to feel it, you just go out into it. If you don't want it, you really have to hide from it.

Robin Johnstone, age 56
Artist, Seattle

Where we seem most effectively to shut out love, it lies covert and concealed; we live not a moment exempt from its influence.

Blaise Pascal (1623–1662)
French mathematician and philosopher

Love is an expression of self. . . . each one of us has creative potential. That creativity can be as simple as a kind word. Fixing a meal. It could be starting a new business. Love is represented by putting our heart and our soul into that creative project—whatever it may be. By putting our heart into something, the effort is like a pebble in a pond rippling out to everything surrounding it.

Fran Don, age 45
Director, Quintile Center, Greenwich, Connecticut

We love too much. . . .

Homer (c. 700 B.C.)
Greek poet

Love is one of those enigmas that man will never understand for one reason only; that it's too human. It causes people to adore, to hate, to take, to give sight, to blind, to give birth and to sacrifice. It is a totally involuntary emotion, beyond the grasp of control. To have a world that is totally controllable is to have a world without love. Love started this world, it will also end it.

Matthew P. McConnell, age 15
Rome, New York

How do I love thee? Let me count the ways.
I love thee to the depth and breadth and height
My soul can reach, when feeling out of sight
For the ends of Being and ideal Grace.

Elizabeth Barrett Browning (1806–1861)
English poet

It's when indescribable happiness reaches through unspeakable loneliness.

Chris Hardy, age 34
Entertainment executive, New York City

There is no happiness comparable to that of the first handclasp when one asks: "Do you love me?" and the other replies, "Yes."

Guy de Maupassant (1850–1893)
French writer

Loving someone is giving them freedom. With children, it's obvious, you give them the tools and skills they need so they can live their own lives. With your spouse and friends, it's giving them the freedom to be who they really are versus who you want them to be. Artists also give us freedom. The arts can free us to see the world in a new way, to see our selves in a new way. When an artist shares of him or herself, they give you an opportunity through their gifts to see, to understand, to feel. That's freedom. That's love.

Ruth Shepard, age 47
Vice-president of communications, United Way of Pulaski County, Little Rock

The thing about love is that it's always new when you see it. Love doesn't fade or become worn out. It has an infinite quality about it and comes in many colors. It surprisingly moves you and edifies you and breaks away crystalline barnacles off you. It's most marvelous when you see it in simple quiet and almost secret acts. It makes you feel hopeful. It's almost like hearing a whisper or seeing a glimpse of eternity.

Adrian Swets, age 67
Architectural designer and contractor, Grand Rapids, Michigan

Love sees what no eye sees; love hears what no ear hears.

John Caspar Lavater (1741–1801)
German writer

Love is finding the familiar dear.

Mona Van Duyn, age 71
U.S. Poet Laureate

Love is in your heart. You just have to take it out.

John Kaneklides, age 7
Charlotte, North Carolina